# tattoos on my soul

Poetry by

## Charles Lemar
# Brown

Broken
Press

## DEDICATION

To the Poet in All of Us

# CONTENTS

# INTRODUCTION

We all have them whether we like it or not. Little mementos of the good times and the bad, of sadness and of joy, of discovery and of loss, of innocence and of heartaches - they are the tattoos on our souls. Some are beautiful, others seem grotesque, but each of them makes us the person we see when we look into the mirror. A collection of scars, some black faded to gray with age, that we try to hide away, others bright and cheerful that we happily display. And if we are lucky and live long enough, our souls will be completely covered. A beautiful mosaic of experiences, some wonderful, some devastating.

It is my belief that if we could see the tattoos of others, we would be a kinder more empathetic species. For I believe if the tattoos on our souls were visible, we would quickly realize that we are more alike than we are willing to admit. And while each of our souls is truly unique, many of the tattoos on them are similar because much of the happiness and the misery, many of the joys and woes, loves and heartbreaks, are emotions we have all experienced.

What better way to record such emotions than to tattoo them on one's soul? And what better way to take those tattoos and show them to the world than through poetry? This volume of poems is dedicated to – the poet in all of us – because we all have tattoos and therefore, we all have poetry in our souls. Some of us choose to share it with the world while others hold it close and dear. There is nothing wrong with either choice. Our tattoos and our poems are our own to do with as we see fit, but I strongly believe that we all have tattoos on our souls and deep inside each of us there lives a poet.

## tattoos on my soul

Shattered and cracked,
Like antique glass,
Wounds that have scarred
Somewhere in the past.
Healed but still broken.
Broken but still breathing,
Fighting the memories
Of love and its leaving.
Beautiful or grotesque?
Sometimes it's hard to know,
What people think when they see,
The tattoos on my soul.

Black ink on white cloth,
The contrast so clear.
One speaks of hope,
The other screams of fear.
I look into the mirror.
The answer is never clear.
Beautiful or grotesque?
Is it neither or both,
When they look at
The tattoos on my soul?

## The Muse

I didn't ask for one.
Didn't search for
One on Amazon,
Or ask a team
Member at
Walmart if they
Stocked them.

Nope, it just
Showed up one
Day and stayed.
I'm not complaining,
Just explaining,
How I came to
Have a Muse.

It's still a mystery
To me as how it works,
It did not come with
Instructions you see.
As a matter of fact
It didn't even come
In a box,
It just showed up
One day and stayed.

Some days it
Bugs me all of
My waking hours,
And sometimes
It sleeps for weeks.
Just sits in the corner
Of the room,
Curled up like
An insolent cat
Refusing to budge.

But on good days,
The two of us play,
And when that happens
Amazing, wonderful things
Materialize, and I remember
How blessed I am, that
It showed up one day
And stayed.

## Simply Complicated

*She's gone it's that simple.*
*It's Time to move on.*
"But it's complicated,"
I say with a frown.

*It's over man,*
*Accept the fact,*
*She ain't never*
*Coming back.*

"I've accepted it,
But I'd rather stay home."
*Oh, I see, I guess*
*You're okay with*
*Growing old alone.*

"I'm busy,
And it's complicated.
I don't have time to date."
*I see, you'd rather set the bench*
*Than actually participate.*

"You think it's simple?
"You think I like it?"
*I think you're scared,*
*Scared as shit.*

"No, I'm not,
And you're being an ass!"
*And you're being a pussy,*
*Living in the past!*

"We're done!
I'm tired of talking to you."
*Well, that's too bad,*
*Cause I am you,*
*And you are me,*
*Looks like neither*
*Of us will ever be free.*

## Prescription Addiction

Last night I had a headache
In my big toe,
And a stomachache in my hair,
And no, I wasn't drinking or smoking,
Or munching on gummy bears.

And This morning when I woke up,
I felt much the same,
Except I also had a toothache
In the middle of my brain.

Now I'm no doctor,
At least I don't think I am,
But I'm starting to wonder
If this is all a scam.

You see, I see,
On my little tv,
A thousand drugs
That will all set me free.

They enter my brain on waves,
Through my ears and eyes,
And make me feel
So healthy and wise.

Side effect you ask -
Oh, I could give you a list,
But not to worry,
They're worth the bliss.

And besides if one occurs,
They make a pill for that.
Oh, hundreds and thousands,
Some big and round,
Some small and flat.

Fear not, you'll be alright,
Hell, I take twenty-seven
In the morning, and another
Seventeen at night.

But they still haven't made one
For the stomachache in my hair,
The doctor says it's because
That condition is really rare.

Oh, I'm sorry.
Am I boring you?
Keeping you from your day?
No worries, it's time for me to take another round of pills.
So, I guess I better be on my way.

## Loneliness Is . .

Loneliness is a box,
With no lid and no light.
It wraps itself around you,
And squeezes with all its might.

Loneliness is a mirror,
Faceless and dark,
That you look into
And pray for light,
Even the smallest spark.

Loneliness is shattered glass.
Loneliness is a broken heart.
Loneliness is deafening silence,
And a world torn apart.

The beginning of the end,
Of the present and the past.
The start of a future,
That you know won't last.

A disease,
A cancer
Without a cure,
Of this
I am sure.
It cares not
If you're young
Or old,
Rich or
Poor,
If you
Are a fallen
Angel, or
If your heart
Is pure.

It does not consider,
Genre, church, or race.
It's only purpose is to spread,
And erase, hope and love and faith,
Until the lidless box implodes,
And the faceless mirror breaks,
Leaving behind a soulless world,
That knows not why it aches.

# Why?

A million scabs,
And I picked them all,
Exposing a heart
Jagged and raw.
I watched the
Black blood
Seep and run,
Until it completely
covered the sun,
And darkness
Like a
Curtain fell,
And all I could do
Was cry and yell
Why!?
Why not let
It heal?
Why not let
It seal
Away the hurt
The anger
The agony
The pain.
Why must we
Expose it again and again?

The past is the past,
It's over right?
At least I thought
It was until tonight,
And with a single word,
The scabs began to fall,
Exposing my peace
And stealing it all,
And in the darkness,
I choked, I cried,
And screamed aloud
Why? Why? Why?

## Between Now and Never

I stand before
You now
and say,
I would never,
I will never,
I swear it,
Swear it forever.
But a lot can happen,
Between now and never.

You see forever,
Is ten years, or
Twenty, or sixty,
But it is not,
Nor will it ever be
Eternity,
So, think hard,
Before you swear forever,
Because a lot can happen,
Between now and forever.

And thus, we come to never,
And those things we would not do.
We say them, think them,
And we know them to be true.

But who knows the future?
And what will be or not?
Ah, but in the moment of truth,
Sometimes never is forgot,
And to preserve our
Bodies, souls, and minds,
It becomes necessary,
To leave never and forever, somewhere behind.
So, before you swear to either,
Never or forever,
Remember, a lot can happen,
Between now and never.

## Anyone But Me

Too big too small,
Too short too tall,
Add an inch, or maybe two,
Drop some pounds, more than a few,
A bigger chest and bigger arms,
Oh, and a six pack,
Yes, that'll set me free
Cause all I really want to be
Is anyone but me.

Too serious, too funny,
Too poor, (laugh) yeah show me the money,
Too fat, too thin,
Too lost, you win,
Now set me free,
Cause all I really want to be
Is anyone but me.

I look in the mirror,
And the mirror looks back,
It does not see what I have,
Only what I lack.
It does not see the beauty inside.
It does not see the pain I hide.
It only sees the outer strife,
And the way I hate my very life,
And it refuses to set me free,
Or let me be what I really want to be,
Anyone but me.

So, for those of you,
Who meet me on the street,
And see a head hung down
In sad defeat,
Please realize that
If I were you,
And you were me,
You too would wish
To be anyone but me.

## Fade Away

There are times,
When the walls press in,
And my mind goes numb,
And the pressure squeezes,
All the happiness from my lungs,
And loneliness pours,
Like a hard winter's rain,
Drenching my body,
My soul, and my brain.
And I wonder,
If the hurting, and
The misery will ever fade,
From the consequences
Of the choices, and the decisions I've made,
Or if all of my tomorrows,
Will mirror today,
And I will simply exist here,
Until I finally fade away.

## The Beginning of Pain

Fireworks explode inside two brains.
Oh, how beautiful the beginning of pain.
The sweet taste of lips,
The slow sway of hips,
Two bodies entwined,
Soul pressed to soul,
Mind inside of mind.
Chaos out of control.
No need to rewind.
Lights fade.
Nothing remains.
The foundation is laid,
The beginning of pain.

## The Bottle

This morning I had a conversation
With the man in the mirror on the shelf.
Nothing all that mind blowing really,
Just me talking to me about myself.
We talked of my youth,
Of every crazy impulse, desire, and whim.
We spoke of the many times
I shook hands with the devil,
As I slowly walked past him.
We reminisced about the women,
And all the fun time we'd had,
But then I recall her, yes her,
The one that nearly drove me mad.
Then I said to the man in the mirror,
"Thank God for forethought and preparation,
Even though she dances through
Our mind as if in celebration,
There is no need to fear
The madness of madness,
For I have here a bottle,
Distilled especially for the eradication
Of seemingly incurable sadness,

And we will drink throughout the day,
Not because we want, but because we must,
And we will stand and fight together,
For it is only you, and me, and this bottle that I trust."
Then I closed my eyes right tight,
And a bit of prayer I said,
Thankful to be alive,
When so oft I should've been dead,
And though I knew I should let it go,
And though I knew it to be a mistake,
Before I turned to walk away,
The bottle I did take.

## My Life Story

Two steps away from happiness,
One step ahead of hell,
That's my life story.
Not much else to tell.

Got my share of brains,
But no extras to pass around.
Got my fair share of looks,
Only worth pennies not Pounds.
Got a car that don't run,
And a boat that won't sail.
That's my life story.
Not much else to tell.

Had me two wives,
Both stayed for a while.
The first took all my money.
The second left with my smile.
Now my kids think I've lost it,
But their young'uns well they think I'm swell.
Yeah, that's my life story,
Not much else to tell.

One day they'll bury me,
Out back in the yard.
I pray it ain't winter,
When the ground is so hard.

Etched in the stone there
Above where I lie,
He lived a good life,
But when he died,
He was two steps from happiness,
And one step ahead of hell.
That's his life's story,
Nothing else left to tell.

## Cupid Sucks

Cupid's arrows fly
Each time you
Catch my eye,
And my eye
You catch quite oft.
"'Twas his aim a
Bit more true
Your heart
Like mine
Might float aloft,
But with each miss,
I miss a kiss,
I never really knew,
And you my love,
Smile and walk away.
No idea. No clue.

A single hit
Is all that's needed.
I've wished and wished.
Hell, I've even pleaded,
But fate just doesn't
Seem to give two fucks.
So, kick rocks I say,
And furthermore,
Cupid Sucks.

## Puppet Me This

Tiny silver strings help us reach life goals.
Little metal wires that sever our souls.
Pull on this one, I look to the right.
Tug on that one, I'm ready to fight.
Oh, and this one, moves my head down and up,
And for an instant I think I'm in love.

What would happen if those strings were cut?
Would life be better?
Or would we all be fucked?

WHAT THE HELL?!! LET'S DO IT!!

No sense just hanging around,
Letting the puppeteer control
The ups and downs.

SNIP! SNIP! Here We Go!
Forever hell or
Eternal bliss,
It's our time now
So, puppet me this.

## Why Not?

I have soar like an eagle,
On the wings of a dove,
Tasted the sweet nectar,
Been drunk on its love.
Felt pure ecstasy,
Falling like rain,
As Cupid's arrow
Removed all my pain.
I've walked valleys low,
Climbed mountains high,
And heard another,
Swear forever, You and I.

But alas, twenty year,
Forever is not,
And who can say,
Why love began to rot.
Or why through the stench
Of failure and defeat,
One heart stopped,
While one heart continued
to beat?

Had the beating heart,
A chance to change the past,
It would not, could not,
Though love did not last.
For, for a moment it held a space,
A wonderful special place,
Where warmth and memories abound,
And deep, deep down,
Some good can still be found.

And so, to answer the question asked,
Tis not in me to love today,
For my days to love have passed.

## Pawns

We are the pawns,
The expendable masses,
On a chess board
That changes as
Each day passes.
The game itself.
Well friends, it's ageless.
And the players,
By choice remain faceless,
As they shuffle us
From square to square,
Leaving us to wonder
Why we are here.
Then a queen swears
We need not worry,
And a king declares
Us all insulate swine,
And the game continues
As the butler pours more wine.
Yes, they push us from place to place
Fucking with our lives and with our mines.
We're simply pawns on a board,
Cogs in a machine,
With an endgame
That is never seen.

One pawn moves.
Another pawn falls.
Each of us ready
At the kings
Beck and call.

NO MORE, I say.
NOT TODAY, I scream.
I will not play
In your asinine scheme.
Today, I stand up
With pawns everywhere.
And United together
We declare.
Today your game ends
And ours begins …

…pawn to e4.
And the game
Begins once more.

## Payday BFF

I won't be with you forever.
That's just how it is my friend,
But you can bet I'll be beside you
Until your last dollar WE spend.

Drinks are on me,
Let me pay for dinner,
Things you'll never
Hear me say,
Yep, I'm just here
To make your wallet thinner.

You're my bestie,
My pal, my numero uno,
My Number one.
I'll be right there with you,
You're financial Siamese twin
Until your bank account
Reaches NONE.
And then I must jet,
Vamoose, twist and spin,
Sianara my friend,
Over and out,
I'm done ...

Oh, it's payday,
You don't say,
My numero uno,
My bestie,
My friend,
And I'm right
At your side,
And here we go
Again …

## LETTING GO

Hope is my anchor,
Faith is my stay,
As I kneel down
   And try to pray.
I grasp hope,
Refusing to be shaken.
Searching for the words
Even as my heart is breaking.
Frustration is constant,
Waves that ebb and flow.
Is it time to stand and fight,
Or time to let him go?

Not my will,
But Thine, Lord,
Not my will,
But Thine,
Words I pray,
Over and over
In my mind.
Hope slips.
My grip tightens.
My soul hurts,
But I keep fightin'.

Is that the river Jordan?
Is that the promised land?
Is the race truly over,
For this righteous man?

I know it's time,
But I can't let go yet.
I need another hour,
Just one more minute.

Lord, give me strength.
Lord, give Dad peace.
I open wide my hand
   And hope release.

## Forever Tonight

It's not you,
And it's not me,
Let's just say
It's destiny.
No, our future
Ain't entwined,
Like our bodies,
And our minds.
So, stay with me,
Just hold me tight,
And know…
Forever is only for tonight.

## Dead Dandelions

There will be no more wishes, my dear.
Someone sprayed the field this year.
Dandelions are weeds you know,
And therefore, will no longer grow.
So, wishing for our wants and needs,
Using their tiny little seeds,
Is now a thing of the past,
And so, I wonder if our love will last,
Or if it's just a crazy myth,
That they hold the magic of a wish,
And paired with an outward breath,
May bestow love, or bring about its death.
And so, as I sit here and ponder,
I cannot help but wonder,
What lies for us ahead,
Since all the dandelions are dead.

## Blow Wishes

Dandelions grew in our
Yard every year,
And children would
Come from far and near,
To make a wish,
And blow the seeds.
Sometimes for wants,
Sometimes for needs.
But always with hope,
That the wish would came true.
Then over time,
The children grew,
And suddenly
To wish,
Well, it became
Childish,
And hope began
To slowly fade,
A day, a year,
a decade,
Passed quickly by,

And Hope thought,
Surely, I will die,
But then just
In the nick of time,
A child made a
Wondrous find,
Held it up and said,
"Mommy what is this?"
A memory formed.
"Oh, my child," the mother
Said, "that is
A blow wish."
And hope sprang
Forth anew,
As the child
Inhaled deeply,
And then blew,
And waited for
Her wish to come true.

# The Lost Key

I once had a key,
But now it is lost.
A key to the closet,
In which I tossed,
The anger and the fury,
The sadness and the pain,
The unbelief and the belief,
The craziness and the strain.

Yes, once I had a key,
It was part of who I was,
But now it is no more,
It is gone because,
I no longer need, the
Things stored behind that door.
I am free.
No longer shackled to the floor.
Free; the burden has lifted,
And a brighter future I see,
Since I locked that door,
And threw away the key.

# Love Poems

I wanted to write love poems,
But that muse flew away.
I think perhaps,
She left with you, on that dreary day.

I did not see her leave,
But I've searched my heart and brain.
I looked in every crack and crevice,
Until I thought myself insane.

Perhaps, she is but misplaced,
I reasoned there at first.
Yet as the days slipped slowly past,
I began to fear the worst.

And now I am almost certain,
She is gone for evermore,
And, so alas, fate has spoken,
I shall write love poems no more.

## *senex nunc*

My granddaughter
Calls it pappy's poop powder.
Pretty close to the truth.
It reminds me
Of the Orange Tang, I drank as a youth,
And I have to wonder,
Why nothing flows as it once
Could,
And what I shouldn't, and
What I should,
Do to ensure proper function
With all the malfunctions
This old body exhibits.
Yeah, Crestor inhibits,
And the Flomax reduces,
While the Cialis induces,
What used to happen
With no help at all.
Now it's fish oil and probiotics,
And B12 if my energy falls.
For brain health it's folate,
And berries, and fish,

Oh, but wait,
I almost forgot Mr. Arthritis,
And how midday naps,
Now tend to excite us.
Some say getting old
Ain't for sissies,
You gotta be tough,
Or so it would seem,
And the alternative,
Well, that's just rough,
If you know what I mean.
So, it's poop powder, and
Supplements, and twice a day pills,
Little plastic organizers to mind us,
And pharmacy bills.
Oh, but please, don't mistake
This for whining,
I'm really alright,
Just thought from
An old man in the
Middle of the night.

## Happiness Remembered

Happiness is a
Beast with little white wings.
It caresses and undresses,
And then it stings.

The heart is a cage,
Where happiness resides.
A hopeless bloody place,
Where love goes to die.

Happiness and the heart,
So misunderstood.
Never portrayed as bad,
Always billed as good,
But 'tis the heart,
That leads the mind astray,
And 'tis happiness,
That encourages us to play,
Forgetting the future and the past.
Be happy,
Just live for today,
Is what happiness will say,
But then tomorrow rolls in
Like a great gray cloud,
With cold sharp rain
thundering loud,
Hiding the sun,
And the happiness,

Revealing
The heart for what it really is…

A rusted wire cage.
A hard steel case.
A prison where love
Goes to stay,
No longer free
To frolic and dance,
Neutered and spade
Of life's romance.

And happiness,
A distant memory,
A cold dark thing,
no longer caressing,
Left only to sting.

## Insomniac

Toss me a rhyme
For Pete's sake!
Insomnia equals poetry,
And I'm wide awake,
Chasing fireflies
Through my head.
I'm going crazy,
At least that what
They said,
Before they took
My sleep away,
Like curtains
Thrown open at
Noon of day,
Showering my brain
With droplets of
Light,
Keeping me
Up all through the
Night.
I'm just tryin'
To pass the
Time,
So, you there,
Yeah,
You.
Please,
Please, toss
Me a rhyme.

## Forever

Time is an illusion,
Spinning its wheels,
A fantasy,
   A façade,
Slowly it kills,
And you,
   You are my
   Heartbeat,
Flatlined and
   Still,
The darkness
   Behind my
   Eyelids,
The, you
Shouldn't have,
And the you
   never dids,
The it doesn't
   Matter
The it's time to
   Move on,
Because the
   Forever
You promised
Is over and gone.

## Black Cat Dreams

My mother could read a man's dreams.
She was of the old gypsy folk.
There were those who doubted her,
But we knew she was no joke.
Many a night when the moon was high,
And the shadows grew long,
She would set by the campfire,
And sing a sad, sad song,
About black cat dreams,
And the man that did her wrong.

My father I never met.
Mother simply said he was gone.
I knew not if she meant away,
Or buried somewhere yon,
But that he was a scandal,
I had not a single doubt,
For when mother hit the bottle,
The old fiddle would come out,
And she would sing a sad, sad song,
About black cat dreams,
And the man that did her wrong.

Myself, I never dreamed of cats,
Black or otherwise.
My nightmares were living,
And I saw them with wakened eyes.
The means street of my town,
Ran blood red,
And the orphans and widows,
Mourned their dead,
And mother played her fiddle,
As she sang her sad, sad song,
About black cat dreams,
And the man who did her wrong.

When I leave this world,
And arrive at those gates of pearl,
I shall asked 'bout the man,
Who mother's mind unfurled,
For I wish to know for certain,
Why my father did her wrong,
And caused her black cat dreams,
And the love of sad, sad songs.

# The Man I Used To Be

Goodbye, Youth.
Goodbye, Innocence.
The pinnacle of stupidity.
The absolute absence of all good sense.
Hello, Maturity.
Hello, Reality.
How ignorant was the
Man I used to be.

Goodbye, twenties.
Hello, thirties.
The decline of stupidity.
Bring on the responsibility.
Hello, Maturity.
Hello, Reality.
How ignorant was the
Man I used to be.

Goodbye, thirties.
Hello, Middle Age.
Where the metabolism stalls
And the health issues rage.
Fuck, Maturity.
Fuck, Reality.
I want to be the ignorant
Man I used to be.

Goodbye, Middle Age.
Hello … Who gives a shit!
I'm old, and I'm weak,
And when I talk, I spit.
It hurts to walk.
It hurts to sit.
My clothes are too tight,
And my hat doesn't fit,
And sometimes I act,
Like I did when I was three,
So, much for wishing to be the
Man I used to be.

## My Old Man's Wisdom

If you're gonna dance with the devil,
You better have the balls to lead.
Just because you want it,
Does not make it's a need.

A bird in your hand,
Will probably shit on your palm.
If I tell you no,
Don't even fuckin'
Think about askin' your mom.

Abstinence is best,
But stupidity will abound,
So, make sure when it arrives,
There's a condom around.

I wouldn't call it rocket science,
Or a perfect system,
Just tidbits of advice,
Salted with my old man's wisdom.

A nail will hold it in place,
But a screw will make it stronger,
And just like in the bedroom,
Better doesn't always equate with longer.

If a person lies to you,
You can bet they'll do it again,
Best to just move along,
And be done with them.

If you don't like the bed you're in,
Don't make it just leave,
And lying down with dogs,
Ain't the only thing that can give you fleas.

I won't call it brain surgery,
Or the most intellectual system,
Just tidbits of advice,
Salted with my old man's wisdom.

# The Phantom Ring

It's been five years,
And still I feel the weight
Of the wedding ring,
I don't wear anymore,
Anytime a waitress says,
"What can I get for you, Honey?"

It's been five years,
Since the ink dried
On the decree
That said it was over,
And I was free
To move on,
But my heart
Is still parked,
Like an old, wrecked truck
In the impound yard,
Waiting to be towed away,
And crushed.

Maybe in another five years,
I'll find a way to fill the hole
That has only grown wider
And deeper.
The hole whose
Edges are jagged,
Like Constantine wire,
Warning off anyone
Who dares to get too close.

Maybe in another five years,
The pain will fade
To a dull numbness,
And the phantom weight
Of the missing ring
Will dissipate,
Or maybe,
I will carry
It with me
Until the heaviness
Of it crushes
My heart and my soul.

# The Contented Heart

The soft kiss of peace,
The warm embrace of hope,
Mercy's caress,
The knot at the end of the rope.

The thudunk-thudunk
That sounds in my chest,
The calm that breaks the storm,
And gives my spirit rest.

My strength, my courage,
The fountain from which
All good starts,
You are my everything,
You are my contented heart.

# The Sound of Silence

A vacuum of absence,
A clash of innocence,
A moment of fear,
Nothing here to hear,
Move along.

Wind through a tree,
The hum of a bee,
Sound disappears,
Nothing here to hear,
It doesn't belong.

A single tear rolls,
Across a tattered soul,
The sound draws near,
A moment of fear,
Nothing here to hear,
End of song.

## LIFE

Seize the moment!
    Grab the hour!
Inhale it like
    The fragrant flower.
Do not stroll,
    Or drag your feet.
Life's too short.
    Life's too sweet.
In time the rose
    Will wither and die,
And the eagle
    Will lose the will to fly.
Now! Now is the time!
    You have the power!
So, seize the moment!
    Grab the hour!

## Poetry Starts

Lightning strikes a broken heart,
Red flowing blood
Turns to black
Turns to words
That become poetry.

Black ink flows
Onto white paper
Turning words
Into poetry
That strikes a broken heart,
Lightning,
Thunder,
Then the rain begins to start.

Tears on pavement,
Drops of bright red blood
Flow from a broken heart,
Perhaps this is where poetry starts.

# JUST SO YOU KNOW

Just so you know,
Eyesight aint' always
The first thing to go.
Sometimes it's the
Little valve that holds
In number one.
Oh, but wait,
We're not even done.
Yeah, believe me when
I tell you,
Because this can also
Be true,
Sometimes it's the muscle,
That holds in number two.

Or it could be the hearing,
Or the taste or the smell,
Or perhaps even the hip
You broke the last time you fell.
A cornucopia from which
Your body may choose,
And when it does
You're the one to lose.

So, whatever it is
That's first to go,
Please understand,
It's important you know,
It won't be the last,
No – not even close.
Like changing your clothes,
It's just a matter of time,
Until nothing quite fits,
And you're losing your mind,
And everyone knows,
Because it all starts to sag,
Or creak,
    Or moan,
        Or whine.

So, chin up,
Chest out,
Shoulders back,
Onward smiling
We go.
It is what it is.
I just thought you should know.

# THE CIRCUS

Every four years,
As routinely as the moon,
The great elites gather,
To plot our annual doom.
'Tis a festive event,
And like sheep we flock,
To watch as the wolves,
Kiss ass and talk their talk.

Oh, the stunts they are amazing,
Though we've seen them all before,
Once again, we sit in awe,
And wonder what's in store,
As an elephant in a tutu,
Dances a political jig,
Promises tax decreases,
And tells of a deficit big,
And an ass in opposition,
Not to be out-classed,
Gathers in his herd,
And they all get fucking smashed.

Yes, a festive occasion, indeed,
They pull out all the stops,
And come November 5th,
We poor ignorant sops,
Gather for the slaughter,
In booths from shore to shore,
And cast our ballets for the butcher,
Who next we shall endure …

…And thus another circus,
Draws slowly to an end,
And we the sheep wander off,
Knowing we've just been fucked again.

# Remember Us Better

Such a brief span,
A mere trickle of sand
In eternity's glass
Into which we spin
righteous and sin
As we slowly waltz past.
In the blink of an eye
We stroll by
A date, a dash, then,
Ashes in the wind.
Oh, but from afar,
As we ascend
Into the stars,
I pray you will
Remember us better
Than we are.

## Wild, Woolly, And Hard To Curry

Six feet even in socked feet.
Hard eyes the color of whiskey neat.
Bowed legs, shoulders broad and wide.
He's been roped but never tied.
Straight forward with purpose,
But never in a hurry,
He's wild, wooly, and hard
To curry.

So, ladies if by chance you meet,
This ole cowboy on the street,
And you think to yourself,
"I'd like that one all to myself."
You should think again,
Or you might be sorry,
Cause he's wild, wooly,
And hard to curry.

# Fingerprints

My soul left,
My body grew cold,
Dead but still living,
Soon to grow old.

Is it murder or theft,
When love is taken?
When love is gone,
And one's life shaken?

I do not know,
Though I will admit,
'Twas here she did
A violent act commit.

Their hearts were stolen,
I've heard others claim,
But mine she left behind,
So 'tis easy to place the blame,
Since my life fell apart,
For you see, she left
Her fingerprints on my shattered heart.

## Dracula Black

Lost souls float through
Eternity and back,
Searching for light
In the Dracula Black.

White fangs, red blood,
There's no turning back,
Once you step
Into the Dracula Black.

Oh, my lady in red,
I must ask,
Will you walk
With me into that black.

Forever together,
Never turning back,
Embracing the darkness
Of the Dracula Black.

## Some Days Are Bad

Some days are bad,
Other days are worse,
Hell and heartache,
Mixed with a curse.
A cocktail of lonely,
Shaken not stirred,
Until reality fades,
And all the lines are blurred...

Memories are real,
The Truth is not,
In this very moment
You are not forgot,
For I hear your voice,
And I see your face,
You are with me
Here in this place.
And in this instant,
All sadness is gone,
Life is good
And you are home.

They say we're
Never really apart,
As long as you
Are here in my heart,
But my heart
Is not my arms, not my bed,
And so 'tis here
My mind has fled,
To the memories of us
Behind these closed eyes,
Where I curse reality,
And hold tight the lies,
That the memories
Are truth, are real,
That you somehow,
Are here with me still.

Then I open my eyes -
Hell and heartache,
Mixed with a curse,
Some days are bad,
Other days are just worse.

# Love Liver

The drink I drank
Made me drunk,
The more I drunk
The more I thunk,
About the liver,
About the heart,
And how each
Has its part,
But more than that
I wondered why,
Then like a baby
I began to cry.
A blubbering fool
I was just then,
Letting out
All from within,
Questioning why
We store love in the heart,
And watch it shatter,
When our worlds fall apart.

Why? I ask,
Are we not more clever,
Why do we not
Store love in the liver?
After all the liver
Itself can heal,
So, unlike the heart,
A broken liver is no big deal.
Just a crazy thought,
From a blubbering fool,
I figured I'd put it out there,
So, you could ponder it too.

## Dream Dancing

I close my eyes,
And bye and bye,
The music begins
To play.
It's our song,
But it's all wrong,
And then it ends,
Just fades away.

Callused hands,
Blows that land,
Blisters begin
To rise
On callused hearts,
The aching starts,
No one wins,
Tear filled eyes.

Midnight dreams,
Or so it seems,
They always win.
Dancing with my ex.
I know what's next,
Nightmares again.

Not tonight,
I must fight,
I need the sleep,
Nightmares again,
They always win,
I begin to weep.
I know what comes next,
When I'm dancing with my ex.

## Dare to Dance

The tune,
Foreign, yet familiar,
Strange, but mesmerizing,
As I sound out the
Measures,
I wonder,
Do I
Dare to dance?

The chorus,
Lively, and promising,
Fearful, but excited,
As I measure the
Pleasure,
I think,
I shall
Dare to dance.

The last verse,
Recognition at last,
Music from the past,
As I walk away,
I know,
That I
Dare not dance.

# Formaldehyde

Heart Pumps!!
Oh, what a ride!!
My veins are
Filled with
Formaldehyde.

Crow's feet? Botox!
Until Nothing slides,
Fill my veins with
Formaldehyde.

Forget the Spanx,
And all they hide,
Just fill my veins
With formaldehyde.

Depressed? Prozac!
And all is fine.
It flows through my veins
Like formaldehyde.

You say it's poison.
You say it's insanity.
Nothing's wrong,
Just conceit and vanity.

But I say,
Keep me young,
Until I die,
Then fill my veins
With formaldehyde.

# Where Is Dead?

An hour from right here,
Two minutes from there,
Out past the galaxies,
In the middle of nowhere.

I ask my dad once
What time it was,
After a smile
And a pause,
He said half
Past a freckle,
A quarter to a hair,
Sometimes I wonder,
If maybe dead could be there.

How do you explain
It to a child so young?
Do you tell them Heaven
Or on a star it's hung?
And what emotion
Does it elicit,
When they ask
If they can go and visit?

Out past the freckles,
And just past a hair,
Where is dead?
It's Somewhere out there…

## Bit By Bit

I lost myself
Littles by little,
Until the pieces
Like breadcrumbs
Marked my path.

It was not my plan,
Not my desire,
To have chunks
Of myself removed,
And tossed aside
Like worthless
Scraps of trash.

So, bit by bit,
Piece by piece,
Little by little,
I collected
Each crumb,
Each chunk,
Each scrap,

And slowly,
Over time
I molded them
Into place,
Until I found
What I had lost,
Myself…

# There was a moment

There was a moment
When I knew what love was,
held it in my hands,
Pressed it to my heart,
Loved it with my all my soul.

There was a moment
When I knew what pain was,
Felt it deep within my soul,
As it pierced my shattered heart,
Burned my eyes and
Seared my throat.

There was a moment
When I forgot what love was,
When fear darkened
My sight like a moonless night,
And my soul screamed,
And my heart hid in fright.

And then,
There was that moment
When you appeared,
And the pain vanished
Like morning dew,
And all I could see was
Me and you,
And once again,
I remembered what
Love was…

## Healing

The worst part of healing,
Is not that you must begin
With a wound.
It is not the pain of having
Your heart and soul stitched
And stabled back together.

The worst part of healing
Is the sleepless nights,
Because the bed is too big.
It's the 'how's it goin's
And the 'how have you been's.
It's the quiet moments,
When you can't get out
Of your own head,
And the 'what if' run
Through your brain
Like rabid squirrels
On an endless loop.
It's the hopelessness.
The terror.
The realization,
That the future
Will come whether
You want it to or not,
Whether you are
Ready for it or not.
It is the fear that
The light at the end of
End of the tunnel
Is not freedom,

But a train
Filled with
Sorrow and
Regret,
That will
Fail to see
You there on
The tracks of
Life.
No, the worst part of healing,
Is not the wound.
The worst part of healing,
Is the healing itself.

## True Love

I looked for you until
The Spring had past,
And the weeping clouds had
cried their last.

I looked for you
Through Summer's heat,
A shimmering mirage,
Of scalding sand
Beneath my feet.

I looked for you until
Autumn had past,
And falling leaves
Covered the path.

Then Winter set in,
And the cold wind blew,
And in that moment,
With clarity I knew,
That you were buried
Somewhere beneath the snow,
And even though I had looked for you,
You were someone I would never know.

## The Goodbye Hurt

The goodbye hurt,
But the betrayal hurt more,
The broken vows,
The forever no more.

Yeah, the goodbye hurt,
But from that I'll heal.
It's the other scars,
That are too deep
Too real.

And so, I thank you, my dear,
Even though we did not work,
For now I know,
That there is something even worse
Than the goodbye hurt.

## Between Two Eternities

Dashes on headstones,
Between two eternities,
Small indications, of
The short journeys,
That proves we're
equal after all.

Walk softly on that dash.
Dare to be bold, but not rash,
For the bell will toll,
As you breathe your last,
And you will know we're
Equal after all.

Alpha and Omega.
And the tiny space within.
Fighting all the way.
In a race we'll never win.
Often, we forget realities,
believe the absurdities,
For we are all equal
In that dash,
Between the two eternities.

## Silence

The silence meant
More to me than
A hundred thousand
Words…

It meant that we
Were broken and
And my soul
Would hurt.

The silence was louder
Than rolling thunder.
It pierced my soul
And tore it asunder.

Each moment of that silence
Was an eternity,
And with each eternity,
We lost a bit
More of you and me,
Until the thunder left,
And the silence reigned,
And nothing of
You and I remained.

Now I sit in silence,
Not lonely but alone,
And enjoy a peace,
I had never known,
And although there
Are times I miss
The thunder and the pain,
I've no desire to feel
That kind of silence again.

## I Still Dream

I still dream about
The good times,
Even though my
Head knows they're gone.
I still dream about you and me,
Every time my heart
Hears our favorite song.
I still dream that
Some day, all will be right,
But then I awaken
At dawn's first light,
And stare at the pillow
Empty there by my side,
And sometimes
I dream that I do not cry.

## One Goodbye

You never said goodbye
Before you left.
You said I love you,
And I had no doubt
You did.

But goodbye and
I love you are not the same,
And while I know you loved me,
The hurt still remains.

Like the clouds I can see,
But cannot touch,
You are gone, but
I still feel your love,
And think perhaps,
You did not say goodbye,
Because you knew one goodbye
Would not have been enough.

## One Day

Maybe one day
I'll hold my head up high,
And smile and laugh,
And enjoy the bright blue sky.

Maybe one day
I won't look down,
Stare at the ground
And wonder why.

Why do I feel this way?
Why is the sky always gray?
Why is my smile always fake?
How much more of this can I take?

Will it happen tomorrow?
Or even later today?
Probably not I think,
But maybe one day.

## The Moment

The moment I let go,
Peace fell like rain
And watered my soul.

The moment I let go,
The clouds rolled away
And my heart began to glow.

The moment I let go,
The sun shone brighter,
My mind became quieter,
And love began to grow.

I still miss you greatly,
But I thought you should know,
That I am living once again,
Since the moment I let go.

## The Digger

If I had a spirit animal,
It would have to be a badger,
Ferocious when pushed,
And a natural digger of holes.

As a digger, I seldom
Know when to stop.
Rock bottom to me
Is just a new beginning,
The edge of the next
Layer of stupidity.

And with any luck,
If I continue to dig,
One day I'll find it.
It being the trap door
That leads to the other side.

Maybe, there I will find peace,
Or perhaps insanity,
But then again,
Knowing myself as I do,
It's more likely
I'll find a shovel,
A fresh piece of ground,
And I'll start digging again.

# Rewrite

Even if I could,
I wouldn't start at the beginning.
That part I like just as it was.
The flirting, the awkwardness,
The holding hands, that first kiss.
No need for edits in those chapters

There are, however, some small changes
I would make in the middle of the book.
I would Revise a paragraph here,
Replace a comma there,
Maybe delete a scene or two,
And I would definitely add more love.

But those final chapters,
Those I would scrap entirely,
And rewrite them completely.
Those chapters I would fill with love,
Every page,
Every paragraph,
Every line.

And I would make sure
That the story ended
As it should have been ended,
With the phrase
And they lived
Happily Ever After…

## Bury The Past

The windshield is bigger
Than the review they said,
Don't look back
eyes straight ahead,
One step forward,
Never step back,
It's about time you
Buried the past.

They didn't say how.
They didn't say where.
So, I used the tools at hand,
And scattered it here and there.

I buried the hatred
   Up on a full moon,
Using a kitchen knife
   And a rusty old spoon.
The anger I hid
   On a beach beneath the sand,
Using only the strength
   Of my own two hands.
The hurt and disgust,
   I left in a mountain glade,
In a deep, deep hole,
   I dug out with an axe and a spade,
But the love,
Oh, the love,
That I buried in the center of my heart,
So, we would never be apart.

# Darkness

Standing in the sunlight,
Surrounded by darkness,
Struggling with demons,
Fighting the madness,
Knowing that despair
Is not reserved for dark places.
Seeing the pitch black
In those forgotten faces,
That frequent lonely corners,
And deserted alleyways,
Where the lost walk,
Or sit, or lay,
And wait for the light
They no longer can see,
As the shadows press forward,
And hope doth recede,
Leaving behind a landscape,
So bleak, so stark,
And the knowledge that
Darkness does not need the dark.

## If Only

If only the sky wasn't blue.
If only I didn't still love you.
If only I could move on.
If only I thought we were through.

If only the sea wasn't so deep.
If only you were mine to keep.
If only I didn't dream of you
Every night when I fall asleep.

If only the ifs weren't only.
If only I wasn't so lonely.
If only I didn't feel like
You're the one that still owns me.

If only breakups were swift.
If only time would heal this rift,
In my heart, and mind, and soul,
Then I could be whole, but only if,
And if only…

# I Found You

I found you broken,
A thousand shattered pieces.
I gathered you up, every last sliver,
And placed you in my heart,
Hoping that time would heal you,
And like a puzzle, the pieces
Would come together again,
And you would be whole.

But time did not heal you,
And I could not heal you,
And my heart grew weary
Of the cuts and scraps,
Caused by the sharp pieces
That were you.
And finally, the wounds
Caused by those shattered pieces
Were just too much, and
The holes in my heart grew large enough,
That sliver by sliver,
The pieces I had gathered, slipped away.

Yes, you were broken when I found you,
And I'm sorry to say,
We were broken when I walked away.

## No Option To Buy

A mansion or a studio loft,
It's all temporary,
We're just renting here,
No option to buy.
One big lease
With unknown terms
In a world where
Uncertainty reigns supreme,
And no matter the
Interest rate or
The size of the dream,
Remember folks,
We're just renting here,
With no option to buy.

Today it's here,
Tomorrow it's all gone.
Repossessed,
Or paid in full doesn't
Really matter, because
We're just renting here,
With not option to buy.

So, put a little kindness
In your bank.
Cash in that certificate.
Deposit some compassion,
Because it's not the house,
The cars, the land,
Those all stay in the end
And then...
We realize we're just renting here,
With no option to buy.

## The Asshole

I ain't no martyr,
I ain't no saint,
Beneath the scrotum,
Behind the taint,
Yeah, I'm the asshole
That they paint.

No use denying,
No use lying,
It is what it is,
I'm just clarifying,
That I'm an asshole,
And I can be trying.

For some it's a body part,
For me it's who I am.
It's my whole persona,
It's my groove, it's my jam.
Oh, and your opinion of me,
Doesn't mean a tinker's damn.

I'm not here to brag,
I'm not here to whine,
Just setting the world straight,
One poetic line at a time,
Yep, I'm an asshole,
And I like myself just fine.

So, if you find me too abrasive,
Or if you find me too brash,
My suggestion would be,
That you move your ass
On down the road
Before the two of us clash,
Because, you see I'm an asshole,
And you, I can tell, are only an ass.

## Fightin' 'em Alone

Ain't nothing' but a thing,
Listenin' to 'em scream,
Nashin' their teeth,
Fill in' me with doubt
About what my life's about,
Tryin' to turn my soul to stone.
I'm fightin' 'em all alone.

Horned and hooved,
And straight from hell,
It's time for round two,
Someone ring the fuckin' bell,
Ain't no time to sit in the corner,
Fuck the shatter heart, the broken bones,
Just let me in the ring,
I'll fight 'em all alone.

Win, lose, or draw,
I may stumble,
But I refuse to fall,
Y'all see this ain't
My first battle,
Probably, ain't gonna be my last,
Yeah, I've fought these
Demons in the past.

And yeah, I wear
Their scars,
But I've left them with
A few along the way,
And I'll keep fightin' 'em
All the long day.
Cause it's the only way
To keep 'em from turnin'
My soul to stone.
That's why I'm out here
Fightin' these demons alone.

## Echoes

Echoes in an empty room.
Silent thoughts that never
Reach the lips.
Clouds but no rain.
Wounds with no pain.
Scars that won't heal.
Hearts that don't feel.
Poems that don't rhyme,
Except from time to time.
Alone, but not lonely,
Or lonely but not alone.
The lights are on,
But no love is home.
Once a king high
Upon a throne,
Now a jester
Beneath a granite stone.
Life well lived, or
Simple existence?
Let us ponder
That for an instance.
For one day soon,
We shall be no more than
Echoes in an empty room.

## Growth

The ground was hard,
Covered with ice and snow.
The air was frigid,
Nothing would grow.

There I planted my heart,
Safe from hurt, from pain.
Confident in my choice,
I smiled, and walked away.

But cold grounds thaw,
And snows melt away,
And where I planted my heart,
A tree grew one day.

And beneath its branches,
My soul was awakened,
And the fear, and the fright,
Was suddenly shaken.

And I looked out
At a bright new day,
And thought to myself,
Perhaps all will be okay.

## Blades of Grass

Fight the rainbow
And Dr. Seuss
And take away a woman's
Right to choose
Yep it's Political Bullshit
For the WIN
And once again
Everyone weighs in
Because what
Are we if not
Predictable
Who cares if
The whole system
Is despicable
It's tradition
That's the way it's
They say
what would
Jesus do
But who really
Listens to Him
After all
They all
Go to church
So they know wrong
From right
At least on
Sunday morning
And sometimes
Wednesday nights.

Shout Hallelujah and Amen
Listen up
You women and you men
Up On Society's
Mount Sinai
Hidden from
Thine eye
The carnal gods on high
Smile and nod
And sigh
At us pitiful masses
So far below
Their asses
Worshiping
Down in the street
Wait for history
To repeat
And wondering why
Nothing changes
But only rearranges
Like Walmart aisles
Every four years
And we bitch and we gripe
And then we wipe our tears
And search for canned goods
On aisle number ten
And the carnal gods
Smile and grin
Knowing they've
Just distracted us once again
Yes that's us

The rich man's
Cannon fodder
And about the
Time we tire of
The slaughter
Another election
Year rolls around
And we forget
The blood there
On the ground
And begin to fuss and bicker
Over our choice of puppets
And they laugh and snicker
And slowly fill our buckets
Once again
Yep, political bullshit for the win

So, we grease the
Wheels of their success
With our
Toil and blood and sweat
And then struggle
To keep our families
Fed and dressed
Beneath their
Bureaucratic net
Beneath their magnifying glass
Uncle Walt was right
We are but leaves of grass
Upon which to trod
And shit and piss

Because after all
It is what it is

And so we smile
And stoop and bow
While they tell us
When and how
We the people
Down below
Should think and speak
And what to know
Just another day
Just another dollar
No need to fret
No need to holler
Tomorrow will be better
Just give it a little more time
While they figure out
More ways to fuck with our minds

But then what can we do
We simple blades of grass
We are only the very foundation
Of the future and the past
The substance in which those
Upon the hill
Their banks and bellies
And pockets fill…

*charles lemar brown*

Oh, but dare we refuse
And stand up at last
Or simply let our future
Mirror our past
Are we the generation
That begins to kick some ass
Or are we just
Your normal every
Generation blades of grass

## The Crystal Ball

Not the future I had planned.
Not one I could understand.
One look into that dark abyss,
And all we built, just dismissed.
A thousand friends, a thousand and one,
But in the end it only took one.
A worm, a fungus, a parasite,
And soon we began to fight.
In the end it all went up in smoke,
Like twenty years was some kind of joke.
Forever together, happily after all,
Yeah right, fuck social media,
And it's amazing crystal ball.

## LETTER TO THE READERS

To You, The Readers,

First and foremost, **Thank You**. Sharing the poems in this book completes the cycle. Without you reading them, the cycle would have been broken. And whether, you found sadness, happiness, or loneliness in the poems, I hope you found a favorite and that it made you feel... for causing feelings is what a poem is meant to do.

And like writing poetry, dealing with one's feelings is a process. For some that process is easy, for others, like me, it is more difficult. In December of 2023, my family buried my Dad, and the process of grieving and healing began. Within this volume are poems that I wrote during that process and the irony of that is this... my Dad was the one responsible for bestowing in me the love of poetry. So, it is with a mixture of pleasure and sadness that I extend a heartfelt Thank You to my Dad. You are missed.

In closing, I would like to address once again the dedication page of this work. In each of us there is a poet. Sometimes the poet is hidden so deep one does not even realize it is there, but given enough time and enough emotion, the poet will arise. In others, the poet floats just beneath the skin and begs to be heard. But whether it is the soft voice of reason, or a blaring trumpet of rebellion brought on by demons only you can see, inside each of us is a poet and that is why this one is dedicated – to the poet it all of us.

Until Next Time,
Charles Lemar Brown

## ABOUT THE AUTHOR

One Pen – Endless Possibilities. I cannot think of a better way to describe my writing. Born and raised in Southern Oklahoma by a high school English teacher and a newspaper columnist, there was little doubt that at some point I would turn to words for comfort. Surrounded on all sides of my family by spinners of yarns and tellers of tales, there was little hope that I myself would not become a storyteller. I am a retired high school science teacher, who now spends much of his time writing and traveling. In addition to this work, I have published three novels, *The Road to Nowhere*, *The Neon Church Journal*, and *The Seventh Date*, two book of short stories entitled *Raised Redneck, Vol. 1 & Vol. 2*, as well as, as a collection of poetry entitled, *heart breaks and cannon fodder*. I live in rural Love County, Oklahoma, where, when not writing, I enjoy spending time with his seven children and twenty-one grandchildren. My favorite quote is—what doesn't kill you makes you stronger and I ain't dead yet.